DISCOVER

SHARKS

Titles in the *Discover Animals* series:

Discover Big Cats
ISBN-13: 978-0-7660-3473-0
ISBN-10:   0-7660-3473-9

Discover Bugs
ISBN-13: 978-0-7660-3472-3
ISBN-10:   0-7660-3472-0

Discover Sharks
ISBN-13: 978-0-7660-3474-7
ISBN-10:   0-7660-3474-7

Discover Snakes
ISBN-13: 978-0-7660-3471-6
ISBN-10:   0-7660-3471-2

DISCOVER
SHARKS

Monalisa Sengupta

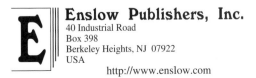

Enslow Publishers, Inc.
40 Industrial Road
Box 398
Berkeley Heights, NJ 07922
USA

http://www.enslow.com

This edition published in 2009 by Enslow Publishers, Inc.

Library of Congress Cataloging-in-Publication Data

Sengupta, Monalisa.
Discover sharks / Monalisa Sengupta.
p. cm. — (Discover animals)
Previously published: [S.I.] : Really Useful Map Company, c2005.
Includes bibliographical references and index.
Summary: "Readers will learn about sharks from the prehistoric
megalodon to the great white and mako sharks today"—Provided by
publisher.
ISBN 978-0-7660-3474-7
1. Sharks—Juvenile literature. I. Title.
QL638.9.S444 2009
597.3—dc22

2008013866

Printed in China

10 9 8 7 6 5 4 3 2 1

To Our Readers: We have done our best to make sure all Internet Addresses in this book were active and appropriate when we went to press. However, the author and the publisher have no control over and assume no liability for the material available on those Internet sites or on other Web sites they may link to. Any comments or suggestions can be sent by e-mail to comments@enslow.com or to the address on the back cover.

Enslow Publishers, Inc., is committed to printing our books on recycled paper.
The paper in every book contains 10% to 30% post-consumer waste (PCW).
The cover board on the outside of each book contains 100% PCW.
Our goal is to do our part to help young people and the environment too!

Photo and Illustration Credits: Q2AMedia

Cover Photos and Illustrations: Q2AMedia

Contents

A Shark's Tale

Sharks are among the most feared creatures on Earth. Found in oceans, seas and rivers, they rule the waters with their sharp teeth and swift movements. Sharks are a type of fish, yet they differ in many ways from other fish.

Bony matters

While most fish have skeletons made of bones, the shark skeleton is made up entirely of cartilage. Cartilage is the same flexible material that is found inside your ears and nose. It makes the shark lighter in weight and helps it to swim faster.

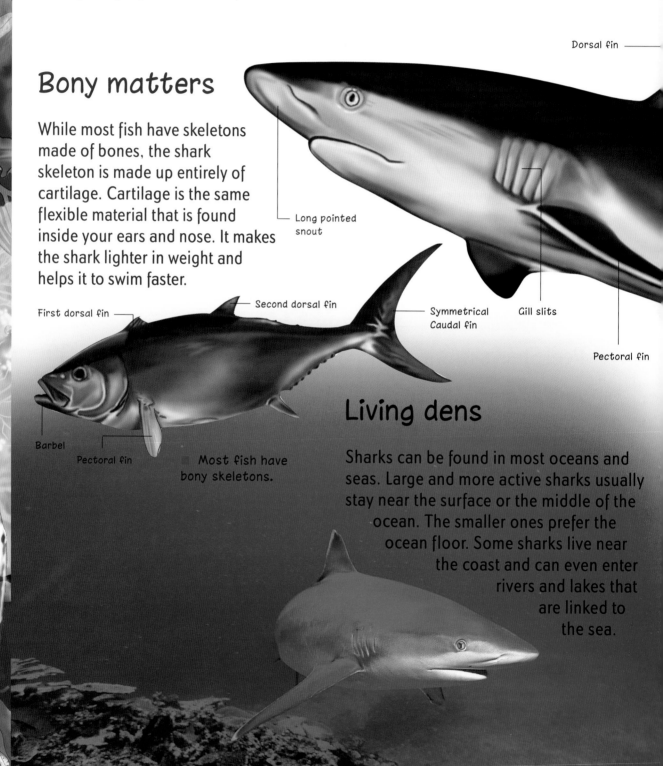

Dorsal fin

Long pointed snout

First dorsal fin

Second dorsal fin

Symmetrical Caudal fin

Gill slits

Pectoral fin

Barbel

Pectoral fin

◼ Most fish have bony skeletons.

Living dens

Sharks can be found in most oceans and seas. Large and more active sharks usually stay near the surface or the middle of the ocean. The smaller ones prefer the ocean floor. Some sharks live near the coast and can even enter rivers and lakes that are linked to the sea.

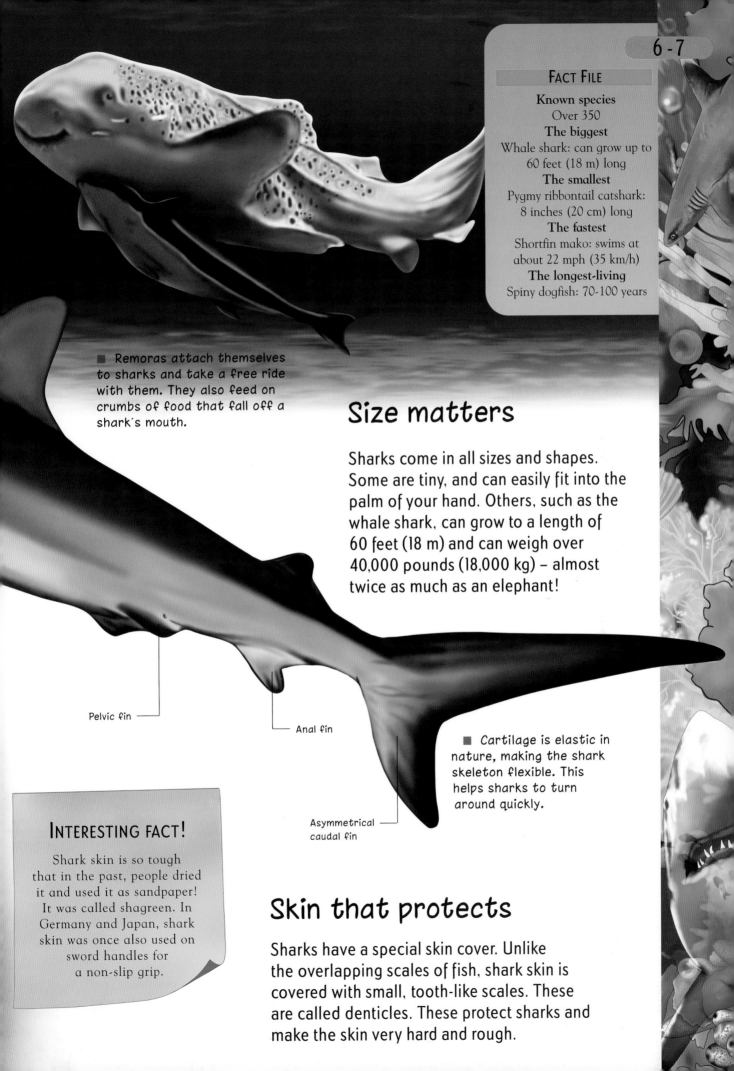

FACT FILE

Known species
Over 350
The biggest
Whale shark: can grow up to
60 feet (18 m) long
The smallest
Pygmy ribbontail catshark:
8 inches (20 cm) long
The fastest
Shortfin mako: swims at
about 22 mph (35 km/h)
The longest-living
Spiny dogfish: 70-100 years

■ Remoras attach themselves to sharks and take a free ride with them. They also feed on crumbs of food that fall off a shark's mouth.

Size matters

Sharks come in all sizes and shapes. Some are tiny, and can easily fit into the palm of your hand. Others, such as the whale shark, can grow to a length of 60 feet (18 m) and can weigh over 40,000 pounds (18,000 kg) – almost twice as much as an elephant!

Pelvic fin

Anal fin

■ Cartilage is elastic in nature, making the shark skeleton flexible. This helps sharks to turn around quickly.

Asymmetrical caudal fin

INTERESTING FACT!

Shark skin is so tough that in the past, people dried it and used it as sandpaper! It was called shagreen. In Germany and Japan, shark skin was once also used on sword handles for a non-slip grip.

Skin that protects

Sharks have a special skin cover. Unlike the overlapping scales of fish, shark skin is covered with small, tooth-like scales. These are called denticles. These protect sharks and make the skin very hard and rough.

The Evolution of Sharks

Most creatures evolve over many generations as their features change to adapt to their environment. But sharks are good survivors and have had little need to change in the last 150 million years.

Few fossils

Fossils are the dead remains of animals that stay preserved for hundreds of millions of years. Fossils have helped us study evolution. But a shark's skeleton crumbles quickly, as it is made of cartilage. Complete shark fossils, therefore, have not been found. All the fossils that have been found have been limited to their teeth and spines from their fins.

■ The Helicoprions lived 250 million years ago. Their jaws had a spiral-tooth setting, with smaller teeth on the front and larger ones at the back.

Earliest sharks

Scientists believe that the ancestors of modern-day sharks appeared 350 to 400 million years ago, a time known as the Age of Fish, or the Devonian Period. This was 100 million years before dinosaurs existed. The earliest shark fossils are found in Antarctica and Australia.

INTERESTING FACT!

It is believed that extinct sharks had short, round snouts, while most modern sharks have long and pointed snouts. Some even have saw-like snouts.

■ The Orthacanthus lived in fresh waters and had V-shaped teeth. This species is now extinct.

■ A Megalodon tooth.

■ A full-grown
human, standing
at 6 feet (1.8 m),
would have been
just as big as the
Megalodon's fin.

The mega monster

One extinct shark known for its huge fossil teeth is the Megalodon.
It lived between 25 and 1.6 million years ago. Each of the
Megalodon's teeth was the size of a full-grown person's hand!
Scientists believe it was probably longer than 53 feet (16 m). It
may have been similar in appearance to the great white shark and
is thought to have fed on whale meat.

Modern sharks

Most modern-day sharks evolved to their present state a long time ago. They have
changed very little in the last 100 million years. But scientists are still not sure
how many kinds of sharks exist today. They continue to discover new species.

Body Basics

Living in the water can be tough. To meet this challenge, sharks are equipped with special features. All sharks have strong jaws, a pair of fins and nostrils and a flexible skeleton. Sharks are great swimmers but, unlike other fish, they cannot move backwards.

Coloring effect

Shark skin is double shaded, with the top side being darker than the belly. When the shark is seen from above, its upper surface appears to resemble the dark ocean floor. Seen from below, the belly blends in with the light above. This helps the shark to hunt without being noticed.

INTERESTING FACT!

A shark's tongue is very different from a human one. Found on the floor of the mouth, it is small, thick and mostly still. It is called a basihyal. Some sharks use it to rip the flesh off their prey.

■ The anatomy of sharks varies according to their habitats. Sharks living in deeper oceans have larger eyes than those found near the ocean surface.

■ Unlike the gills of bony fish, shark gills do not have covers. Water must continue to flow across the gill slits for the shark to breathe.

Gill filaments

Oxygen depleted water

Oxygen rich water

Gill arches

Heart

Ventral aorta

Breathing skills

Sharks, like other fish, take oxygen from water. They have gill slits on either side of their heads. Water enters these slits and passes over the gill chambers, where oxygen is absorbed. Some sharks need to swim continuously to breathe, while others open and close their mouths to pump the water in.

■ Most sharks have five pairs of gills, while bony fish have just one. The broadnose sevengill shark, however, has seven pairs of gills.

Oil Tank!

The largest organ in a shark is the liver, which is filled with oil. Since oil is lighter than water, it helps keep the shark from sinking. Despite this, sharks must swim constantly to keep afloat. The liver also functions as a storehouse of energy.

Torpedo-like!

Most sharks have a rounded body that tapers at both ends. This torpedo-like shape helps them while swimming. But some sharks, like the angelshark, have a flat body. This helps them to live at the bottom of the ocean.

■ Sharks usually have blunt snouts. But sawsharks have long snouts with toothed edges, which help them to dig out prey from the ocean floor or to slash at fish passing by.

■ The unique shape of the hammerhead shark's head helps it to get a better view of its surroundings.

Shark Senses

Sharks have all the senses that humans do – and something extra too! Sharks can not only smell, see, feel, hear and taste. They also have a sixth sense. Their senses help them to hunt and travel great distances.

Surface Pore

Canal

Main Tube

Sensory cells

■ Lateral line canals are lined by tiny hair-like structures. Any movement in the water hits these hair-like structures, causing them to send a message to the brain.

Line of action

Sharks have fluid-filled canals that run from head to tail on both sides of their body. This is called the lateral line. It enables the shark to sense movements in water. Some scientists believe that the lateral line can also detect low sounds.

Sixth sense

All living creatures produce weak electrical fields. Sharks are able to detect these with the help of their sixth sense. Tiny pores on the shark's snout lead to jelly-filled sacs known as the ampullae of Lorenzini that help them detect electrical fields.

Lateral line canal

Smelly matters

In general, the nostrils of sharks are located on the underside of their snouts. They are used for smelling and not for breathing. Some sharks have nasal barbels, which look like thick whiskers sticking out from the bottom of the snout. Barbels help the shark to feel and taste.

■ Blind sharks cannot see. They hunt for their prey by using their nasal barbels.

■ Certain sharks, such as the nurse
shark, have openings called spiracles
just behind their eyes. The spiracles
help increase oxygen to the shark's
brain while hunting or feeding.

Looking on

Sharks have very good eyesight, even better
than ours. Sharks also have a reflective layer
inside their eyes that helps them see better
in dim light. Sharks can also see colors.

INTERESTING FACT!

Sharks do not have
external ear flaps. Instead,
their ears are inside their
heads, on both sides of the
brain case. Each ear leads
to a small pore on the
shark's head.

■ The great white shark has
a keen sense of smell. It can
detect a drop of blood in
25 gallons (95 liters) of water!

Toothy Terrors

A shark's only real weapon is its mouth. The mouth is below the snout in all species except the angelshark, the megamouth, whale shark and wobbegong shark. These species have their mouths at the end of their snouts. The two most important parts of a shark's mouth are the teeth and the jaws.

Tearing and crushing

Sharks do not chew their food, but gulp it down whole. They use their teeth only to tear the food into mouth-sized pieces. Some sharks also crush the shell of their prey with their teeth.

Big bite

In most animals, the lower jaw moves freely, but the upper jaw is attached to the skull. However, in sharks, the upper jaw rests below the skull. It moves out when the shark attacks its prey. This allows the shark to push its entire mouth forward to grab its victim. As the lower jaw teeth puncture and hold the prey, the upper jaw teeth slice it.

■ The great white has large wedge-shaped teeth with jagged edges. The teeth of the Megalodon were three times larger than those of the great white.

Great white shark

Sand tiger

Mako

■ Different types of shark teeth.

Hammerhead

Blue shark

Sharp new ones

Shark teeth fall out all the time. This is crucial, as worn out or broken teeth are continually replaced by new and sharper ones. The process takes place as often as every two weeks. In some sharks, like the great white, these teeth are arranged in several rows.

FACT FILE

Number of teeth
Over 3,000
For a bite
5-15 rows of teeth
Teeth replaced every
10-21 days
Largest tooth is the
Megalodon's, at nearly
6 inches (15 cm)
Bite strength
Average of 25,000 pounds
per square inch

Tooth types

Sharks have a variety of teeth. Some have molar-like teeth, which help in the process of grinding. Others have razor-like cutting or pointed teeth.

■ Cookie-cutter sharks eat their prey by attaching themselves to it with special sucking lips. Once attached, they roll their body to cut out a chunk of flesh!

INTERESTING FACT!

The basking shark has very tiny teeth. It does not use them to feed. Instead, the shark swallows plankton-rich water. Special bristles inside its mouth, called gill rakers, filter this food as the water flows through them.

■ The Port Jackson shark does not have jagged teeth. Its front teeth are pointed for grasping its prey, while the back teeth are flat and molar-like for crushing.

Young

Baby sharks are called pups. A single litter could contain more than 100 pups! There are three different ways in which shark pups are born.

Laying eggs

Some sharks lay eggs like birds. The mother deposits the egg cases in the sea. The baby inside the egg gets its food from the yolk until the egg hatches. The parents do not protect the eggs. Horn sharks and swell sharks are egg-laying sharks. Such sharks are known as oviparous sharks.

Birth of a shark

Sharks like the hammerhead give birth to pups. The eggs hatch inside the mother's body and the babies get their food from the mother directly. Sharks that give birth to their young in this manner are called viviparous sharks. Lemon sharks, hammerheads, bull sharks and whale sharks are all types of viviparous sharks.

■ Horn shark eggs are spiral shaped and hatch six to nine months after being laid. The pups are usually 6-7 inches (15-17 cm) long.

■ Certain shark's eggs are also called mermaid's purses because of their pouch-like appearance. The egg contains yolk that the baby feeds on.

Hatching inside

In some sharks, although the eggs hatch inside the mother, the young do not get nourishment directly from their mother. Instead, the babies feed off other unfertilized eggs. At times, they even eat their brothers and sisters! This kind of reproduction is called ovoviviparity.

■ A shark giving birth. The newborn pup lies on the ocean floor for a while after it's born. It then pulls against the cord that links it to its mother. Once the cord breaks, the young one swims away.

INTERESTING FACT!

Shark eggs are enclosed in a tough leathery membrane. They can be of various shapes— pouch-like or shaped like a screw. Some even have tendrils that attach themselves to seaweed and rocks on the ocean floor.

Caring for babies

Sharks do not care for their babies. The young sharks are well-equipped to look after themselves. In fact, they swim away from their mothers as soon as they are born. Sometimes a mother might even eat her newborn pups.

■ The predators of young sharks include larger sharks and killer whales. Some small sharks are even eaten by huge fish like the giant grouper.

Giants of the Deep

Huge sharks have dominated the oceans of the world for centuries. Although the largest sharks today do not compare in size to the Megalodon, they can still grow to enormous sizes. Among the modern sharks, the largest are the whale shark and basking shark.

Not a whale!

Contrary to what its name suggests, the whale shark is not a whale. It is a shark that can grow to the length of a bus! The whale shark has a huge mouth that may measure up to 4 feet (1.2 m).

Straining food

Whale sharks and basking sharks feed on plankton by straining the tiny marine plants and animals from the water. They swim with their mouths open and suck in water filled with plankton. The shark then filters its food through special bristles attached to the gills and swallows the food. The water is ejected through the gill slits.

INTERESTING FACT!

Both whale sharks and basking sharks are slow swimmers. They swim by moving their body from side to side. Neither of these sharks is a danger to humans.

Whale shark

Colorful skins

Whale sharks have light gray skin with yellow dots and stripes. On the other hand, basking sharks are darker in color. They are grayish-brown to black or blue on the upper surface, while their belly is off-white in color.

FACT FILE

The whale shark can grow as long as 46 feet (14 m)
The basking shark is a close second at 33 feet (10 m)
Whale sharks may live up to 100 years
Basking shark pups are the largest at 5.5 feet (1.7 m)
Whale sharks swim at a speed of 3 mph (4.83 km/h)

■ Whale sharks love fish eggs. They are known to wait for hours for fish to lay eggs so that they can eat them. They even return year after year to the same mating grounds where the fish release their eggs into the water.

■ Basking sharks are named this because they cruise slowly along the ocean surface. This gives them the appearance of basking in the sun.

The big basking shark

The basking shark is the second-largest shark. It has a short and conical snout. Unlike whale sharks that travel alone, basking sharks often move around in schools of 100 members.

Pygmies of the Deep

Not all sharks are huge monsters. Some are, in fact, so small that they can fit into your hand! The smallest sharks include the pygmy ribbontail catshark, dwarf lanternshark and the spined pygmy shark. But like their bigger siblings, small sharks have strong teeth, and a bite from them can be very painful!

Whale shark

Marked bodies

The dwarf lanternshark has strongly marked light and dark areas on the body along with streaks and spots. The skin has slender, needle-shaped denticles. The females are often longer in size than the males.

Bigger tastes

Spined pygmy sharks may be tiny, but they love to eat squid, shrimp, and fish. Their upper teeth are narrow and small, while the lower ones are large and knife-like.

■ The Freycinet's epaulette is a tiny shark found in the coral reefs of Papua New Guinea. It hides during the day and hunts at night.

Tiny and glowing

Spined pygmy sharks are very sleek and have a bulb-like snout. They are dark grey to black in color and have white-tipped fins. Their bellies actually glow in the dark. They live in deep waters and are rarely seen.

FACT FILE

The dwarf lanternshark is 6-8 inches (15-20 cm) long
The spined pygmy shark is 7-8 inches (18-20 cm) long
The Pygmy ribbontail catshark is 6-8 inches (15-20 cm) long
The spined pygmy is found at depths of 6,550 feet (2,000 m)

Epaulette shark

■ The pygmy ribbontail catshark lives on the muddy ocean floor, on slopes and outer shelves. It looks tiny compared to the huge whale shark.

INTERESTING FACT!

Spined pygmy sharks are commonly found at the bottom of the ocean. However, these sharks are known to journey up to about 650 feet (198 m) at night to hunt in the mid-water zones.

Ribbons undersea

Pygmy ribbontail catsharks are dark brown in color with blackish markings on the fins. They are found around Tanzania, India, Vietnam and the Philippines. The small shark feeds on small bony fish and crustaceans.

The Great White Shark

Infamous for its appearance in the movie *Jaws* as a bloodthirsty man-eater, the great white shark is the largest predatory shark. The name *Jaws* was fitting, given that this shark has as many as 3,000 razor-sharp teeth! It grows to over 15 feet (4.5 m) in length and weighs as much as 3,000 pounds (1,360 kg)! The great white is also known as the "white pointer" and "white death."

Where are they found?

Great white sharks live in temperate to warm waters. They are found across the world – from the coasts of America, the Gulf, Hawaii, South Africa and West Africa to Scandinavia, the Mediterranean Sea, Australia, New Zealand, Japan, and the eastern coastline of China and southern Russia.

Color that helps

The great white is actually gray or bluish-gray in color, with a white underbelly. Its coloring helps it to get close to its prey without being noticed. When seen from below, the white underbelly blends in with the bright reflection of the sky. Quite often, this shark attacks its victims by sneaking up quietly. The shark's grayish color then helps it to blend in with the dark water.

■ Great white sharks are solitary creatures and prefer to swim alone. However, they have sometimes been sighted in pairs.

Fierce bite

With a mouth that is most often open, you cannot miss the rows of white, triangle-shaped, razor-sharp teeth. The shark's teeth can grow up to 3 inches (7.5 cm) long. Old or broken teeth are replaced by teeth from the next row.

HABITAT

FACT FILE

Average length
12-16 feet (3.6-4.9 m)
Can grow up to
22 feet (6.8 m)
Can be as heavy as
7,300 pounds (3,312 kg)
Number of babies
2-14 pups
Shark attack
30-50 attacks per year
Fatal attacks
10-15 deaths every year
Can swim as deep as
3000 feet (900 m)

INTERESTING FACT!

Great white sharks are ovoviviparous. The eggs of the great white remain inside the body of the female shark until they hatch. The female then gives birth to live young.

■ Great white sharks often jump out of the water while chasing seals. This is called breaching.

What do they eat?

■ Great whites are known to attack pelicans, but they prefer to eat seals.

Great whites eat dolphins, sea lions, seals, big bony fish and even penguins. Though they have earned a reputation for being man-eaters, they do not usually attack humans as prey. These sharks are also scavengers, as they eat dead animals that float in the water.

The great white first attacks its victim, injures it and then moves away. It approaches it later, when the pain and bleeding has weakened it. The shark does not chew its food, but rips the prey into mouth-sized pieces before swallowing them. After a good meal, the shark can do without another one for over a month!

Tiger Sharks and Bull Sharks

Many sharks, like the tiger and bull sharks, are named after land animals. The tiger shark has dark stripes on its back, similar to the big cat. But as the shark grows older, the stripes often fade away. The bull shark gets its name from its flat, wide and short snout, which resembles that of a bull.

■ Tiger sharks have good eyesight, which is aided by a special gill slit called a spiracle. Located behind the eye, this slit provides oxygen directly to the eyes and the brain.

Tough tigers

The tiger shark has a very large mouth with powerful jaws. The triangular teeth of these sharks have saw-like edges that can slice through many objects. The tiger shark is not a very fast swimmer and often hunts at night.

Junk eaters

Tiger sharks love food and will eat almost anything. Biologists have found alarm clocks, tin cans, deer antlers and even shoes in the stomachs of dead tiger sharks! Tiger sharks also feed on other sharks, fish, turtles and crabs.

■ Tiger sharks often prey on albatross chicks, which fall into the ocean while learning to fly.

Bull sharks

The bull shark lives near coastal areas. It also sometimes enters into rivers and freshwater lakes. Bull sharks eat fish, other sharks, turtles, birds and dolphins. As with many sharks, adult female bull sharks are longer in size than male bull sharks.

Danger zone

It is dangerous to go near bull and tiger sharks, as they are known to be man-eaters. Tiger sharks are the second-most threatening species to humans, after the great white. Bull sharks rank third in this respect.

INTERESTING FACT!

Bull sharks travel from the upper Amazon River to the sea every season. They cover a distance of 2,300 miles (3,700 km) during this journey.

■ Bull sharks have hardly any predators. But there have been reports of crocodiles eating bull sharks.

The Swift Mako

Sharks are great swimmers, and the fastest among them is the mako. The mako's speed has been recorded at 31 mph (50 km/h). The mako is known for its ability to leap out of the water, to heights of up to 20 ft (6 m). They have even been known to jump into boats!

Shaped for speed

Makos are fast swimmers because of their sleek, spindle-like shape. They also have a long and conical snout. Their side fins are short and the tail fin is crescent-shaped to provide more power while swimming.

Other relatives

Makos belong to the order of mackerel sharks. Other sharks in this order include the great white, the porbeagle and the sand tiger shark. Sand tiger sharks are also called grey nurse sharks. They are found in most warm seas around the world. The porbeagle gets its name from its porpoise-like shape.

■ The sand tiger shark is known to swim to the surface and take huge gulps of air. It holds the air in its stomach to lie motionless in the water.

HABITAT

FACT FILE

Can be as heavy as
1000 pounds (450 kg)
Average length
9-12 feet (2.7-3.7 m)
Number of pups in a litter:
10-12
Size of pups
28 inches (71 cm)
Capable of swimming at
46 mph (74 km/h) in bursts

On the hook

Makos are a popular sport fish. When hooked, they jump around, making them harder to catch. Although makos rarely attack humans, they can be dangerous.

On the menu

Most makos live in warm waters. They feed on bluefish, herring, mackerel and swordfish. Their teeth are long, thin and sharp. This enables makos to catch slippery fish. You can see their teeth even when their mouths are shut!

Dolphins

INTERESTING FACT!

Like most sharks, makos are double shaded. Their upper body is deep blue in color, while the sides and the belly are white. The blue shade helps the mako to camouflage itself while hunting.

■ Larger makos can eat swordfish, marlins and even dolphins.

Ground Sharks

Ground sharks are the most common type of sharks. They have long snouts and a mouth that reaches behind the eyes. Their eyes are special too. Ground shark eyes have a lower eyelid that moves to cover the eyes during hunting. Ground sharks include hammerhead, carpet and swell sharks and all the requiem sharks, such as the tiger, blue, lemon, bull and certain reef sharks.

Lemon shark

Yellow fellows

The lemon shark gets its name from its deep yellow-brown color. But its belly is off-white. This shark hunts mostly at night. During the day, it loves to laze on the ocean floor.

Blue moods

The blue shark has a slim body that is deep blue on the back, bright blue on the sides and white on the belly. They also have slender snouts and large eyes. They are the second-fastest swimmers after the mako. While there were once many blue sharks in the ocean, over-fishing has led to a drop in their population.

■ The nictitating membrane of the blue shark helps it to protect its eyes while hunting.

■ The swell shark can increase the size of its body by swallowing large amounts of water. This scares away the shark's enemies.

Danger factor

Lemon sharks live near the surface and are often seen at bays, docks and river mouths. Though they swim close to human areas, lemon sharks rarely attack unless provoked. Meanwhile, blue sharks live far away from the shore, and yet are known to attack humans.

INTERESTING FACT!

The blue shark migrates the longest distances—typically 1,200-1,700 miles (2,000-3,000 km). The record is a 3,700 mile journey from the New York area to Brazil!

■ While most sharks eat other sea animals, California sea lions love to feed on young blue sharks.

No fuss about food

Blue sharks can eat anything, but they prefer squid and fish. On the other hand, the lemon shark likes to feed on crabs, rays, shrimp, sea birds and smaller sharks.

Reef Sharks

Sharks live in different zones and regions of the ocean. Some, such as blacktip, whitetip and Caribbean reef sharks, live near coral reefs. Divers and waders often come into contact with such sharks.

■ Whitetip reef sharks are viviparous. A single litter could contain between one and five pups. Each pup is around 24 inches (61 cm) long.

White cousins

The whitetip reef shark is gray in color, with white tips on its dorsal fin and tail. It is slender and has a broad head. It feeds mainly on bony fish, octopuses, lobsters and crabs.

Sleepy sharks

Caribbean reef sharks live near the coral reefs of the Caribbean. These sharks often appear to be asleep as they lie motionless at the bottom of the ocean. They love to feed on bony fish.

The blacktip

The blacktip reef shark is very interesting to look at. Its body is gray in color, but the tips of its fins are black. The shark also has a white streak on its side. The blacktip reef shark thrives in aquariums.

INTERESTING FACT!

Whitetip reef sharks are most active at night, when they roam the reef in search of food. During the day, the shark rests in coral caves. Whitetips rest in groups, but they hunt alone.

Living zones

Reef sharks live in different areas and depths of the ocean. The blacktip reef shark is found on sand flats at depths of 50 feet (15 m). The whitetip prefers to live in corners and caves around coral reefs.

Angelsharks

Angelsharks have flat bodies, which make them look very much like rays. They often bury themselves in sand or mud, leaving just their eyes and the tops of their bodies protruding.

Eye

Spiracle

Pectoral fin

Pelvic fin

Winged sharks

Angelsharks have long, wide fins that look like wings, which is why they are called angelsharks. They have a blunt snout, and their skin color is similar to that of the sand and rocks found in the ocean. This helps them to hide from their prey or enemies.

■ Both angelsharks and rays give birth to live young. They also have similar flat bodies. But unlike rays, the fins of the angelshark are not attached to the sides of its head.

FACT FILE

Can grow up to
6.5 feet (2 m)
Number of babies
8-13 pups
Found at depths of up to
4,300 feet (1,300 m)
Can be as heavy as
60 pounds (27 kg)
Pups born at depths of
60-90 feet (18.3-27.4 m)

Hunting by surprise

The angelshark hides in the sand and rocks, waiting for its prey. As a fish swims by, the shark pounces on it suddenly. The angelshark eats fish, crustaceans and mollusks. It has small, sharp teeth.

First dorsal fin

Caudal fin

Second dorsal fin

INTERESTING FACT!

Angelsharks are not really dangerous if left in peace. But they can bite if you step on them. That's why they are sometimes called sand devils!

Bottom dwellers

Angelsharks live at the bottom of the ocean and prefer warm waters. They are mostly found in the Pacific and Atlantic Oceans. Angelsharks are not fast swimmers, but their prey is often even slower! The angelshark feeds on a variety of reef fish including croakers, groupers and flatfish.

Hammerheads

Hammerhead sharks are unique creatures and can be easily recognized, even from a distance. They have a flat and rectangular head, which resembles a hammer. There are many types of hammerhead sharks. They can be differentiated by the shape of their heads.

Heady features

The eyes of the hammerhead shark are placed at the ends of its distinct head. The eyes can be as far apart as 3.3 feet (1 m), allowing the shark to view a larger area. Its flat head also helps the shark to keep its balance, as its side fins are very short.

Hammerhead Eye

Little differences

The great hammerhead has a straight head with a slight notch in the center. The scalloped hammerhead has rounded corners on its head, while the smooth hammerhead has a broad and flat head without a notch. The bonnethead is smaller, with a shovel-shaped head.

■ The upper side of the hammerhead is dark brown, light gray or even olive in color, while its belly is white.

■ The great hammerhead migrates seasonally, moving to cooler waters during the summer.

FACT FILE

Can grow up to
20 feet (6.1 m)
Can be as heavy as
500 pounds (230 kg)
Can live up to
20-30 years
Found at depths of
1000 feet (305 m)
Number of babies
6-42 pups per litter

INTERESTING FACT!

Angelfish act as official cleaners to hammerhead sharks. They pick up parasites from the sharks' skin and even inside their mouths. Interestingly, the hammerhead does not eat these cleaners!

Home sweet home

Hammerheads can be found across many areas. They can live at depths of 1000 feet (305 m) and can also be found in shallow coastal areas, including lagoons. They are usually found in the Mediterranean Sea and the Atlantic, Pacific and Indian Oceans.

Stingray

Meal time

Hammerhead sharks eat crabs and fish. But their favorite food is stingray. The shark pins the stingray down using its "hammer." It feeds after sundown, and hunts along the seafloor as well as near the surface. Large hammerheads also eat smaller ones.

Sharks with a Difference

The world under the ocean is a curious place. It is home to many living creatures of all shapes, colors and sizes. Sharks also belong to this wonderful world. Ornate wobbegongs, carpet sharks and horn sharks are just some of the odd members of the shark family.

■ The horn shark is not considered to be dangerous to people, but the spines on its dorsal fins can hurt if the shark is handled.

The horned pig

The horn shark has a short and blunt head, and looks very much like a pig! It is either gray or brown in color, with dark spots covering its body. The shark's small teeth are located in the front of its jaw, with large crushing molars along the sides. It is most active at night and feeds on sea urchins, crabs, worms and anemones.

The ornate ocean creature

The ornate wobbegong lives in the Australian and Pacific coastal reefs. It is called ornate because its skin has patterns in brown, yellow and gray colors. This helps the shark to blend into its surroundings.

Baiting for food

The wobbegong has worm-like projections around its mouth. The shark uses these to suck its prey into its mouth. Like the angelshark, the wobbegong also surprises its victims by camouflaging itself at the bottom of the ocean.

■ This varied carpet shark is a relative of the whale shark. But there are very few similarities between the two. The varied carpet shark is small and has a distinctive black "collar" with white spots.

INTERESTING FACT!

The horn shark's egg cases are curiously shaped in a spiral, like a screw. Each case contains one pup and takes from six to nine months to hatch.

The ornate wobbegong

Goblins in water

The goblin shark has an unusual snout, which is long, flat and pointed. The jaws point outward when the shark eats, making it look very peculiar indeed! It has soft, pale pinkish-gray skin.

■ Little is known about goblin sharks, but it is believed that they are slow swimmers.

All in the Family

Sharks have many relatives in the ocean. One of their closest cousins is the ray. Sharks and rays have a common ancestor that lived about 200 million years ago.

■ Skates and rays look very similar. The main difference between them lies in their method of reproduction. Rays are viviparous, while skates lay eggs.

Body matters

The biggest difference between sharks and rays is their body shape. While many sharks have long slender bodies, rays have flattened ones. But some sharks, like angelsharks, have bodies like those of rays.

Gill slits

Similar features

Sharks and rays have many common features. Both have skeletons made of cartilage and skins covered with denticles. Both sharks and rays have between five and seven gill slits. However, a shark's gill slits are on either side of its head, while a ray's gill slits are on the underside of its body.

■ Manta rays may seem scary to look at, and are often called devil rays. But in reality, manta rays are playful and splash around in the water!

Swimming skills

Sea creatures have different styles of swimming. For instance, rays flap their big side fins in order to swim. But sharks use their much smaller fins just for lifting and steering. They use their tails to move around in water.

■ The saw of a young sawfish is covered in a protective membrane to avoid hurting the mother when she gives birth.

Name game

Like many big families, sharks and their relatives may have similar names, as do sawfish and sawsharks. But there are often important differences between them. For example, the sawshark has gill slits on its sides and barbels in the middle of its "saw." The sawfish has gill slits on its underside, and no barbels.

INTERESTING FACT!

Many rays have spines on their tails that can sting other animals. These spines can be poisonous, too. Some rays have long and whip-like tails, while others have shorter ones.

Shark Attack!

Over the years, shark attacks have caught the imagination of film makers and fiction writers. The image of a shark with its huge mouth wide open, flashing its deadly teeth, has thrilled many a movie-goer. But not all sharks are a threat to us.

Not always deadly

Most often, shark attacks do not result in death. Sharks usually only attack humans out of fear. Some attacks are also by accident, when a shark mistakes human surfers for seals!

■ It is not a good idea to swim with an open wound, as the smell of blood attracts sharks.

Be careful

One has to be careful while swimming in shark-inhabited waters. One should always swim during the day and in a group. Leave the water immediately if a shark is spotted, but do so quietly. And never try to grab a shark, even if it is a small one!

ANNUAL DATA

Total shark attacks
75-100
Unprovoked attacks
Around 50
Provoked attacks
15-20
Fatal attacks
11-15
Number of attacks
recorded in US:
over 30 per year

■ Sharks are curious animals. They will survey a man in a cage, even though they cannot attack him!

Warning bells

If you upset a shark by trespassing in its territory, it usually warns you before attacking. It shakes its head and swims with its back hunched and snout point-ing up. This is called agonistic display. If such movements are seen, one should swim away before it's too late.

INTERESTING FACT!

People are more likely to die from bee stings or dog bites than to be killed by sharks! In fact, more than 90 percent of those attacked by sharks manage to survive.

Most dangerous

There are four sharks that are particularly dangerous to humans. These are the great white, tiger, bull and oceanic whitetip sharks. Seventeen other types of sharks have also attacked humans, but they are dangerous only if threat-ened or disturbed. These include lemon, hammerhead, blacktip reef, nurse, wobbegong, sand tiger and spitting sharks.

■ Florida has one of the highest attack rates by the great white in the world, but deaths are very rare. Most of the attacks are on surfers and divers.

Endangered Sharks

Sharks are the kings of the oceans, as they have no natural predators. They have a reputation for being ruthless hunters. But today, sharks have much to fear from humans. Different parts of sharks, such as their skin and fins, are used for various purposes.

In danger

Due to the wide-scale killing of sharks, there has been a drop in the shark population. In fact, many have become endangered. They are so few in number that if we don't stop hunting them certain species could become extinct. To protect such sharks, many countries have made it illegal to kill sharks.

Just a bycatch

Some sharks are caught by accident, as ships and fishermen try to catch other fish. A shark caught in this manner is called a bycatch. People are now working on ways to stop these accidental killings.

INTERESTING FACT!

You can adopt a shark! Adopted sharks are specially tagged, so that you can track their movements. Shark adoption is a great way to support and protect sharks.

■ Sharks usually attack us only if we disturb them, but humans follow and hunt sharks even as a sport.

Many products

Sharks are used in a variety of man-made products. Shark scales are removed from the skin and the hide is used to make a type of leather. The liver oil of some sharks contains large amounts of Vitamin A. Until the late 1940s, such sharks were hunted in large numbers for Vitamin A.

■ Shark-liver oil contains more Vitamin A than cod-liver oil.

■ Shark-liver oil is sometimes used in the manufacture of lipsticks and other cosmetics.

Soupy tales

The Chinese use dried shark fins to make a popular and expensive soup. The best soup is considered a highly prized delicacy, and some restaurants charge as much as $100 a bowl.

■ Fins used in soups are often obtained in a cruel manner. In some countries fishermen drag living sharks from the sea and slice off their fins and tails. The wounded sharks are then thrown back into the water, where they bleed to death.

Glossary

Agonistic display: Territorial behavior of an animal, warning that it is preparing to attack.

Anatomy
The structure of the body of an animal or plant, or any of its parts.

Barbel: Thin, whisker-like organs found near the mouth of certain fish and sharks.

Biologist: A scientist or an expert who studies living organisms.

Bycatch: Fish and other animals caught by accident as fishermen try to catch other fish.

Cartilage: A tough, elastic tissue in the body. A shark's skeleton is made of cartilage; in humans, it is found in the ears and nose.

Crustaceans: Any of the animals, such as crabs, lobsters and shrimp, which belong to the class Crustacea.

Denticles: The small, tooth-like scales on shark skin that help protect the shark and make its skin feel rough.

Evolution: The gradual change in a species over many generations as it adapts to its environment.

Gills: The organ that fish use to breathe.

Illegal: Against the law.

Jaws: The bones inside the mouth in which teeth are attached.

Lagoon: A shallow lake which is cut off from the sea by coral reefs or sand bars.

Liver: A reddish-brown organ in animals that plays an important role in digestion.

Membrane: A thin fibrous tissue that covers or lines cells and organs in animals and plants.

Molar: A tooth that grinds food.

Mollusks: A group of invertebrates including snails, slugs, octopuses, squid, clams and mussels.

Nictitating membrane: A thin fold of skin under the eyelids that can be used to cover the eyes. It is usually found in reptiles, birds and certain mammals.

Oviparous: Animals that lay eggs.

Ovoviviparous: Animals whose eggs develop inside the female's body, hatching just before or just after birth.

Plankton: Tiny plants and animals that drift with the currents in seas and lakes.

Predatory: The tendency or characteristic of an animal to hunt other animals for food.

Remora: A long, flat fish with spiny fins found in the ocean. It attaches itself to other fish and rocks underwater with the help of sucking discs on the top of its head.

Requiem shark: Any shark belonging to the Carcharhinidae family. This includes the tiger shark and the lemon shark.

Scavenger: An animal or bird that feeds on already dead or decaying matter.

Spiracles: Openings behind the eyes of certain sharks that help increase oxygen to the brain while hunting or feeding.

Temperate: Moderate or mild in temperature. Not too cold or too hot.

Tendrils: Long thread-like structures.

Torpedo: A cigar-shaped underwater missile that is usually launched from a submarine, aircraft or ship.

Viviparous: Animals that give birth to live young.

Further Reading

Books

Healy, Nick. *The World's Deadliest Sharks.* Mankato, MN: Capstone Press, 2006.

Savage, Stephen. *Access—Sharks.* New York: Kingfisher, 2007.

Vadon, Catherine. *Meet the Shark.* Minnetonka, Minn.:
Two-Can Publishing, 2007.

Internet Addresses

Just for Kids: Sharks
http://www.flmnh.ufl.edu/fish/Kids/kids.htm

NOVA Online Adventure: Island of the Sharks
http://www.pbs.org/wgbh/nova/sharks/

Shark School
http://www.sdnhm.org/kids/sharks/index.html

Index